ORIGAMI
2004 CALENDAR

**Andrews McMeel
Publishing**

an Andrews McMeel Universal company
Kansas City

www.andrewsmcmeel.com

Photography by Lynton Gardiner

Origami objects are from the exhibition Origami Masterworks, organized and presented by Mingei International Museum in collaboration with OrigamiUSA, October 2003 through January 2004. Guest curator, V'Ann Cornelius.

Mingei International Museum, Inc., Balboa Park, San Diego, California 92101
(619) 239-0003
email: mingei@mingei.org
www.mingei.org

OrigamiUSA, 15 West 77th Street, New York, New York 10024
(212) 769-5635
email: masterworks@origami-usa.org
www.origami-usa.org

Cover: ORIGAMI GRAND DRAGON
designed and folded by
JOSEPH WU
using six sheets of paper

All Jewish holidays begin at sundown the previous day.

ISBN: 0-7407-3798-8

2004

JANUARY

S	M	T	W	T	F	S
				1	2	3
4	5	6	7	8	9	10
11	12	13	14	15	16	17
18	19	20	21	22	23	24
25	26	27	28	29	30	31

FEBRUARY

S	M	T	W	T	F	S
1	2	3	4	5	6	7
8	9	10	11	12	13	14
15	16	17	18	19	20	21
22	23	24	25	26	27	28
29						

MARCH

S	M	T	W	T	F	S
	1	2	3	4	5	6
7	8	9	10	11	12	13
14	15	16	17	18	19	20
21	22	23	24	25	26	27
28	29	30	31			

APRIL

S	M	T	W	T	F	S
				1	2	3
4	5	6	7	8	9	10
11	12	13	14	15	16	17
18	19	20	21	22	23	24
25	26	27	28	29	30	

MAY

S	M	T	W	T	F	S
						1
2	3	4	5	6	7	8
9	10	11	12	13	14	15
16	17	18	19	20	21	22
23	24	25	26	27	28	29
30	31					

JUNE

S	M	T	W	T	F	S
		1	2	3	4	5
6	7	8	9	10	11	12
13	14	15	16	17	18	19
20	21	22	23	24	25	26
27	28	29	30			

JULY

S	M	T	W	T	F	S
				1	2	3
4	5	6	7	8	9	10
11	12	13	14	15	16	17
18	19	20	21	22	23	24
25	26	27	28	29	30	31

AUGUST

S	M	T	W	T	F	S
1	2	3	4	5	6	7
8	9	10	11	12	13	14
15	16	17	18	19	20	21
22	23	24	25	26	27	28
29	30	31				

SEPTEMBER

S	M	T	W	T	F	S
			1	2	3	4
5	6	7	8	9	10	11
12	13	14	15	16	17	18
19	20	21	22	23	24	25
26	27	28	29	30		

OCTOBER

S	M	T	W	T	F	S
					1	2
3	4	5	6	7	8	9
10	11	12	13	14	15	16
17	18	19	20	21	22	23
24	25	26	27	28	29	30
31						

NOVEMBER

S	M	T	W	T	F	S
	1	2	3	4	5	6
7	8	9	10	11	12	13
14	15	16	17	18	19	20
21	22	23	24	25	26	27
28	29	30				

DECEMBER

S	M	T	W	T	F	S
			1	2	3	4
5	6	7	8	9	10	11
12	13	14	15	16	17	18
19	20	21	22	23	24	25
26	27	28	29	30	31	

ORIGAMI CUBE WREATH

designed, folded, and assembled by
BENNETT ARNSTEIN
using 280 sheets of paper

Printed in China. No part of this booklet may be used or reproduced in any manner whatsoever without written permission except in the case of reprints in the context of reviews. For information write Andrews McMeel Publishing, an Andrews McMeel Universal company, 4520 Main Street, Kansas City, Missouri 64111.

www.andrewsmcmeel.com

Diagram Production Manager Marc Kirschenbaum
Diagrams by Atsushi Tajiri

OrigamiUSA, 15 West 77th Street, New York, New York 10024
(212) 769-5635
email: membership@origami-usa.org
www.origami-usa.org

ORIGAMI

PATTERNS

FACETED WATERBOMB

This is a jewel-like version of an ancient traditional model called "waterbomb" because it will hold water. When made from gift-wrapping foil, it is a lovely tree ornament.

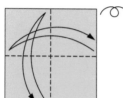

1. Paper square.
   Fold in half like a book.
   Unfold. Repeat in the
   other direction. Turn over.

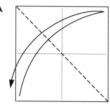

2. Fold in half
   diagonally.
   Unfold.

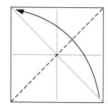

3. Fold in half
   diagonally.

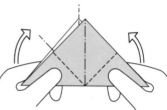

4. Hold by bottom corners and push
   together until the center lines of
   all four sides meet.

5. Press flat with two flaps
   on each side.
   Turn end-for-end.

6. Fold upper layer of
   flaps only.

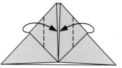

8. Fold corners to center.

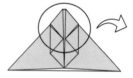

9. The next drawing
   shows only the circled
   area.

Pocket

10. Fold free top corner
    downward, so the outer
    edge fits along edge of
    pocket.

11. Tuck top corner into
    pocket.

12. Repeat steps 10-11
    on the other side.

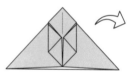

13. Turn over and
    repeat steps 10-12
    on the back.

14. Arrange flaps so they
    stick out in 4 directions.

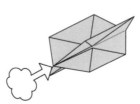

15. Hold gently, with locks on
    top and bottom, not at sides.
    Blow with a strong puff
    into the hole end.

16. Push in the center line
    of each of the square
    areas that radiate from
    the ends, four at the top,
    four at the bottom.

17. Finished.

The cup works. If you want to drink from it, use strong paper.

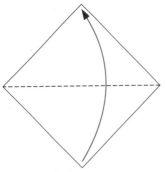

1. Fold in half

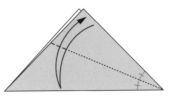

2. Bring one side edge to bottom edge, but don't crease hard. Just pinch where the fold reaches the other side edge. Unfold.

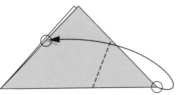

3. Bring the bottom corner over to the pinch mark. Fold hard.

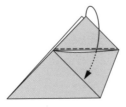

4. See the pocket in the flap you have just made? Fold one layer of paper above the pocket downward and push it into the pocket as far as it will go.

5. Flap is now locked into place. Turn over.

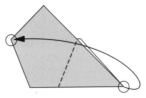

6. Repeat steps 3-4 on this side.

7. Finished Cup!

8. Made of about 20 inches square, the cup becomes a hat!

BLOW-UP BUNNY

1. Paper square.
   Fold in half like a
   book. Unfold.
   Turn it over.

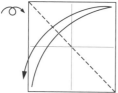

2. Fold in half
   diagonally.
   Unfold.

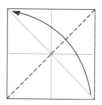

3. Fold in half
   diagonally.

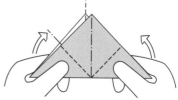

4. Hold by bottom corners and push
   together until the center lines of
   all four sides meet.
   Turn over end-for-end.

5. Fold upper layer of
   flaps only.

6. Fold corners to
   the center.

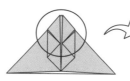

7. The next drawing
   shows only the
   circled area.

8. Fold free top corner
   downward to outer
   edge (to fit along edge
   of pocket).

9. Tuck top corner into pocket.

10. Repeat steps 8-9
    on the other side.

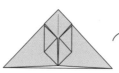

11. Turn over.

12. Bring folded edges to
    center line.

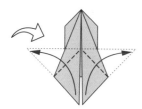

13. Fold ears out to the
    side.

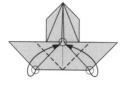

14. Bring outside dots to
    center dots to finish
    the ears.

15. Hold by ears and
    blow in at the tip
    of the nose.

16. Finished Bunny. Shape
    to taste. This is a Chinese
    paperfold.

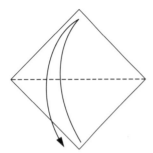
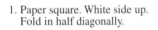

1. Paper square. White side up. Fold in half diagonally.

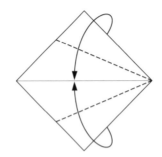

2. Bring two adjacent edges to crease.

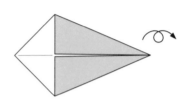

3. Turn over.

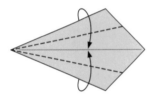

4. Bring folded edges to crease.

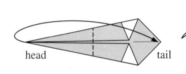

head   tail

5. Bring head to tail.

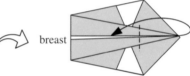

breast

6. Fold head toward breast.

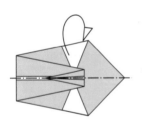

7. Pick up and fold in half downward and toward the rear.

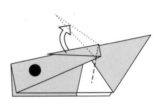

8. Hold at black spot. Pull up head. Pinch back of head to set new crease.

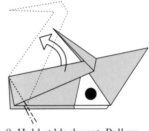

9. Hold at black spot. Pull up neck. Pinch breast to set new crease.

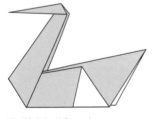

10. Finished Swan!

Makes place cards, gift tags, and mobiles, as well as tree ornaments. Use a needle to put thread through the top of head. Knot the ends to make a loop for hanging the swan.

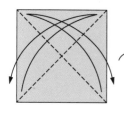
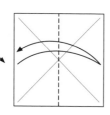
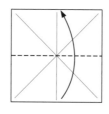
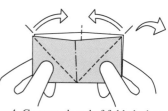

1. Paper square. Fold in half diagonally. Unfold. Repeat in the other direction. Turn over.

2. Fold in half like a book. Unfold.

3. Fold like a book the other way. This time, leave it folded.

4. Grasp each end of folded edge and push hands together until the four corners of the paper meet!

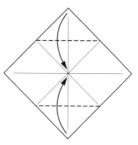
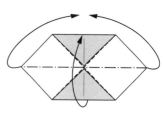

5. Press flat, with two flaps on each side.

6. Now, open everything out.

7. Bring opposite corners to center.

8. Fold up again on the creases you have already made.

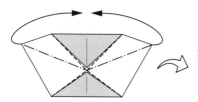

9. Keep going.

10. Turn one sail down over edge of hull.

11. Fold sail back up, making a little pleat at the bottom.

12. Tuck pleat under edge of hull.

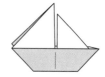

13. Turn it over.

14. Fold up bottom point at hull. This makes a base on which the boat will stand. Turn it over.

15. Finished Boat! Use it as a place card, party favor, or tree ornament.

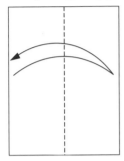

BOX

traditional

Although known among folders as the "magazine cover box," this can made from almost any strong, stiff paper of about the same proportions.

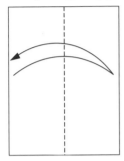

1. Fold in half lengthwise. Unfold.

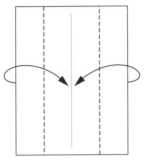

2. Bring longer edges to meet the center crease.

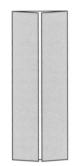

3. Unfold.

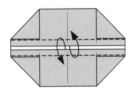

4. Book-fold crosswise. Unfold.

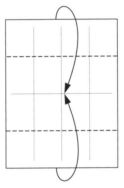

5. Bring the shorter edges to meet at the center crease. This time leave the folds in.

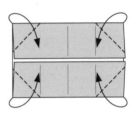

6. At each corner, bring the folded edge to lie along the nearest crease. Note that the cut edges do NOT reach the crosswise center line.

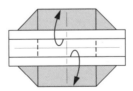

7. Fold the cut edges of the paper outward, one up and one down, as far as you can over the corner flaps to hold them in place.

8. Grasp the edges and pull them up and apart. The ends of the model will fold upward to become the ends of a box. Pinch the corners of the box to make them square.

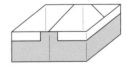

9. Finished Box! Make another for a lid. If you use a magazine cover (front and back), save the prettier one for the lid, and begin with the pretty side down. For very best result, the box should be a little smaller than the lid.

Use a small rectangle of stiff paper. A 3" by 5" file card is just right.

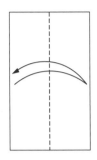
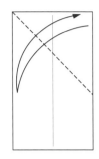
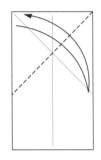
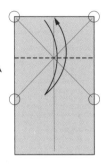

1. Fold in half length-
   wise. Unfold.

2. Bring top edge to
   side edge. Unfold.

3. Bring top edge to
   side edge. Unfold.
   Turn it over.

4. Bring top edge down to
   place where diagonal
   creases reach sides. The
   fold will pass through the
   point where the diagonals
   cross. Unfold. Turn it over.

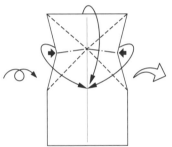

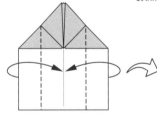
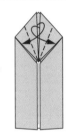

5. Push in the center of paper
   where all the creases intersect.
   The edges will fold up on the
   prepared lines. Push the sides
   inward and the top down on
   top of them. Press flat.

6. Fold the little flaps in
   half upward. They will
   become the front legs.

7. Bring side edges to
   meet at the center
   crease.

8. Fold front leg flaps
   in half downward
   and outward.

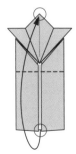

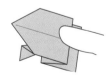

9. Bring bottom edge to
   tip of nose.

10. Fold upper flap in
    half downward.
    Turn it over.

11. Finished Frog!
    Push down on rear edge. As
    finger slips off, frog jumps.
    Can you make her jump into
    a box?

STAR BASKET

A 6-inch square makes an individual nut dish or candy dish.

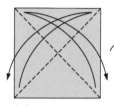

1. Paper square.
   Fold in half diagonally.
   Unfold. Turn it over.

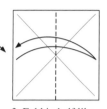

2. Fold in half like a
   book. Unfold.

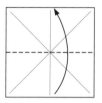

3. Fold like a book the
   other way. This time,
   leave it folded.

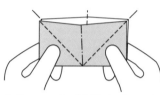

4. Grasp each of folded edge and
   push hands together until the
   four corners of the paper meet.

5. Press flat, with two flaps
   on each side.

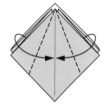

6. Bring the top edges
   of upper flaps to meet
   at center line.

7. Squash to the right.

8. Repeat step 7 on the
   other side.

9. Repeat steps 7-8 on
   the back side.

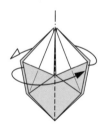

10. Rotate flaps.

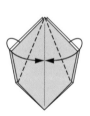

11. Bring top edges of
    upper flaps to meet at
    center line.

12. Fold each corner
    downward.

13. Rotate flaps.

14. Repeat step 12.

15. Basket is now ready to
    be opened out. Spread
    the sides apart. The bottom
    will unfold and flatten
    into a square.

16. Finished Star Basket!
    Fill with something
    tasty.

TREE ORNAMENT WITH SHELVES   by Giuseppe Baggi

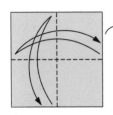

1. Paper square.
Fold in half like a book.
Unfold. Repeat in the
other direction Turn over.

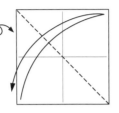

2. Fold in half
diagonally.
Unfold.

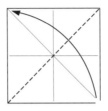

3. Fold in half
diagonally.

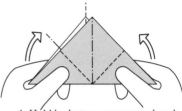

4. Hold by bottom corners and push
together until the center lines of
all four sides meet.

5. Press flat with two flaps
on each side.
Turn end-for-end.

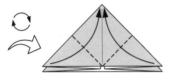

6. Fold upper layer of
flaps only.

7. Fold little flaps in half,
downward.

8. Turn over.

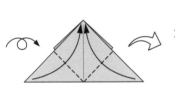

9. Repeat steps 6-7.

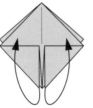

10. Lift little flaps so they
stand straight up.

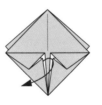

11. Open out top layer
of one flap only.

12. Bring sides of model
together to form a slight
angle. The two little
flaps overlap, with the
closed one inside the
opened one.

13. Push the outer layer of
paper back into place.

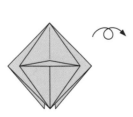

14. The overlapping flaps now
form a shelf. Turn it over.
Repeat steps 10-13.

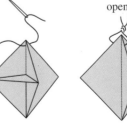

15. Finished Ornament! Use a needle to
put a thread through one end of it.
Knot the ends of the thread to make
a loop for hanging the ornament.

BOX

by Giuseppe Baggi

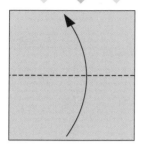

1. Paper square.
   Fold in half like a book.

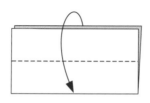

2. Bring top edge to bottom
   edge. Fold both layers.

3. Bring ends to top edge.
   Crease hard and unfold.

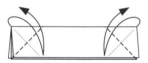

4. Bring ends to bottom edge.
   Crease and unfold.
   Turn it over.

5. Turn ends inward so that
   they meet. Crease hard and
   unfold. Turn it over.

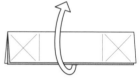

6. Unfold all but the first fold.

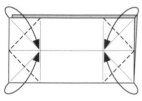

7. Bring all four corners to
   crosswise crease, using
   the crease you have
   already made. At top, fold
   one layer only.

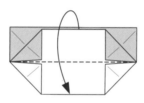

8. Bring top edge of upper
   layer only to the bottom
   edge.

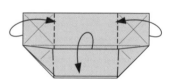

9. Pull lower section straight up.
   The sides will follow. Pinch
   the corners at the front edge
   of your box to make them sharp.

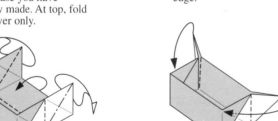

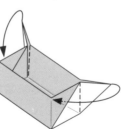

10. At back, pinch corners together
    to form "ears." As you do, the
    back of the box will come up.

11. Wrap ears over the ends of the
    box and tuck them into the
    pockets there.

12. Finished Box! You can make
    it from a rectangle like this
    sheet, and the shape of your
    finished box will be square.

CHAIN

by David Shall

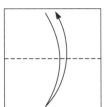

1. Fold in half like a book. Unfold.

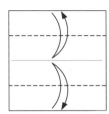

2. Bring side raw edges to meet at the center line. Unfold.

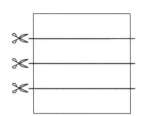

3. Cut along these crease lines. Use scissors or a knife—whichever is easiest for you.

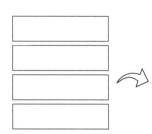

4. You have four rectangular strips (each 4 by 1).

5. Bring end corners together and pinch the fold to make a "landmark."

6. Fold long raw edges to the center landmarks. Don't leave a gap between the edges now at the center. Unfold.

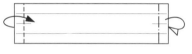

7. Fold the left short raw edge inward so you see a colored rectangle made up of four small squares. Fold backward making a rectangle of four small squares on the other side.

8. Step 7 complete.

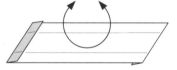

9. Side view. Roll into a ring and hook the end flaps together.

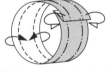

10. With the end flaps hooked together, line up the edges and creases. Hold the over-lapped flaps tightly and fold the raw edges of both sides to the inside using existing crease from step 6.

11. Beginning with the overlapped flap area, curl and smooth to give the line a nice round shape. Now, make a chain!

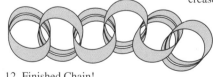

12. Finished Chain!

LETTER FOLD

by David Shall

Use a rectangle. If you intend to mail this, use an 11" by 14" (legal size) paper to meet postal standards.

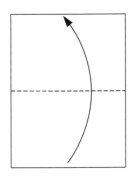

1. Written side up.
   Fold in half.
   Leave folded.

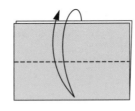

2. Fold in half again.
   Unfold.

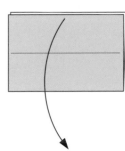

3. Unfold again.

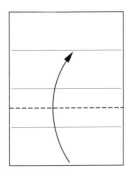

4. Bring bottom edge to
   third fold. Leave folded.

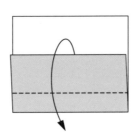

5. Bring the same edge downward, using the fold you
   already have.

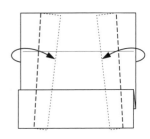

6. Fold in each side, starting
   each fold a bit slanted.

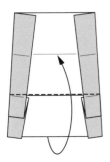

7. Fold up the bottom third.

8. Fold down the top third
   and tuck it in the pocket.

9. Finished letterfold!
   Turn it over.

10. Write to someone
    special today!

**Andrews McMeel
Publishing**

an Andrews McMeel Universal company

4520 Main Street, Kansas City, Missouri 64111
www.andrewsmcmeel.com
Copyright © 2003 OrigamiUSA
Printed in China

DECEMBER 2003

S	M	T	W	T	F	S
	1	2	3	4	5	6
7	8	9	10	11	12	13
14	15	16	17	18	19	20
21	22	23	24	25	26	27
28	29	30	31			

JANUARY 2004

S	M	T	W	T	F	S
				1	2	3
4	5	6	7	8	9	10
11	12	13	14	15	16	17
18	19	20	21	22	23	24
25	26	27	28	29	30	31

MONDAY 29

TUESDAY 30

WEDNESDAY 31

THURSDAY 1

New Year's Day
Kwanzaa ends (USA)

FRIDAY 2

Day after New Year's Day (NZ)
Bank Holiday (Scotland)

SATURDAY 3

SUNDAY 4

ORIGAMI SISTERS

designed and folded by
GIANG DINH using one
sheet of handmade paper

JANUARY 2004

S	M	T	W	T	F	S
				1	2	3
4	5	6	7	8	9	10
11	12	13	14	15	16	17
18	19	20	21	22	23	24
25	26	27	28	29	30	31

JANUARY

MONDAY   5

TUESDAY   6

WEDNESDAY   7

THURSDAY   8

FRIDAY   9

SATURDAY   10   SUNDAY   11

ORIGAMI ANKYLOSAUR

designed and folded by
SATOSHI KAMIYA

using one sheet of handmade paper

JANUARY 2004

S	M	T	W	T	F	S
				1	2	3
4	5	6	7	8	9	10
11	12	13	14	15	16	17
18	19	20	21	22	23	24
25	26	27	28	29	30	31

JANUARY

MONDAY 12

TUESDAY 13

WEDNESDAY 14

THURSDAY 15

FRIDAY 16

SATURDAY 17

SUNDAY 18

ORIGAMI TESSELATION 1A

designed and folded by
CHRIS PALMER
using one sheet of paper

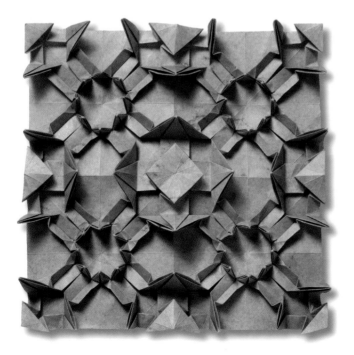

ORIGAMI TESSELATION 1B

designed and folded by
CHRIS PALMER
using one sheet of paper

JANUARY 2004

S	M	T	W	T	F	S
				1	2	3
4	5	6	7	8	9	10
11	12	13	14	15	16	17
18	19	20	21	22	23	24
25	26	27	28	29	30	31

MONDAY 19

Martin Luther King Jr.'s Birthday (observed) (USA)

TUESDAY 20

WEDNESDAY 21

THURSDAY 22

FRIDAY 23

SATURDAY 24

SUNDAY 25

JANUARY 2004

S	M	T	W	T	F	S
				1	2	3
4	5	6	7	8	9	10
11	12	13	14	15	16	17
18	19	20	21	22	23	24
25	26	27	28	29	30	31

FEBRUARY 2004

S	M	T	W	T	F	S
1	2	3	4	5	6	7
8	9	10	11	12	13	14
15	16	17	18	19	20	21
22	23	24	25	26	27	28
29						

MONDAY 26

Australia Day

TUESDAY 27

WEDNESDAY 28

THURSDAY 29

FRIDAY 30

SATURDAY 31

SUNDAY 1

FEBRUARY 2004

S	M	T	W	T	F	S
1	2	3	4	5	6	7
8	9	10	11	12	13	14
15	16	17	18	19	20	21
22	23	24	25	26	27	28
29						

FEBRUARY

MONDAY

2

Groundhog Day (USA)

TUESDAY

3

WEDNESDAY

4

THURSDAY

5

FRIDAY

6

Waitangi Day (NZ)

SATURDAY

7

SUNDAY

8

ORIGAMI CENTAUR

designed and folded by
TAKASHI HOJYO

using one sheet of paper

FEBRUARY 2004

S	M	T	W	T	F	S
1	2	3	4	5	6	7
8	9	10	11	12	13	14
15	16	17	18	19	20	21
22	23	24	25	26	27	28
29						

FEBRUARY

MONDAY

9

TUESDAY

10

WEDNESDAY

11

THURSDAY

12

FRIDAY

13

SATURDAY

14

St. Valentine's Day

SUNDAY

15

ORIGAMI MASK – BROWN
designed and folded by
ERIC JOISEL
using one sheet of dampened paper

FEBRUARY 2004

S	M	T	W	T	F	S
1	2	3	4	5	6	7
8	9	10	11	12	13	14
15	16	17	18	19	20	21
22	23	24	25	26	27	28
29						

FEBRUARY

MONDAY   16

Presidents' Day (USA)

TUESDAY   17

WEDNESDAY   18

THURSDAY   19

FRIDAY   20

SATURDAY   21   SUNDAY   22

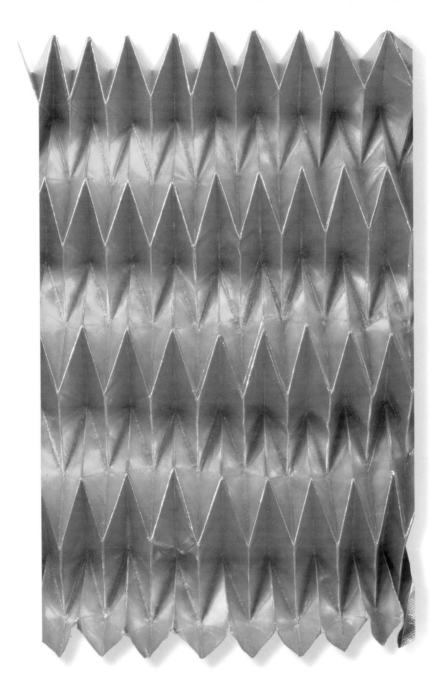

ORIGAMI PLEAT FORM – GOLD

designed and folded by
FLORENCE TEMKO
using one sheet of paper

FEBRUARY 2004

S	M	T	W	T	F	S
1	2	3	4	5	6	7
8	9	10	11	12	13	14
15	16	17	18	19	20	21
22	23	24	25	26	27	28
29						

FEBRUARY

MONDAY 23

TUESDAY 24

WEDNESDAY 25

Ash Wednesday

THURSDAY 26

FRIDAY 27

SATURDAY 28

SUNDAY 29

ORIGAMI BOWL
designed and folded by
PAUL JACKSON
using one sheet of textured paper

MARCH 2004

S	M	T	W	T	F	S
	1	2	3	4	5	6
7	8	9	10	11	12	13
14	15	16	17	18	19	20
21	22	23	24	25	26	27
28	29	30	31			

MARCH

MONDAY 1

St. David's Day (UK)
Labour Day (Australia—WA)
Eight Hours Day (Australia—TAS)

TUESDAY 2

WEDNESDAY 3

THURSDAY 4

FRIDAY 5

SATURDAY 6

SUNDAY 7

Purim

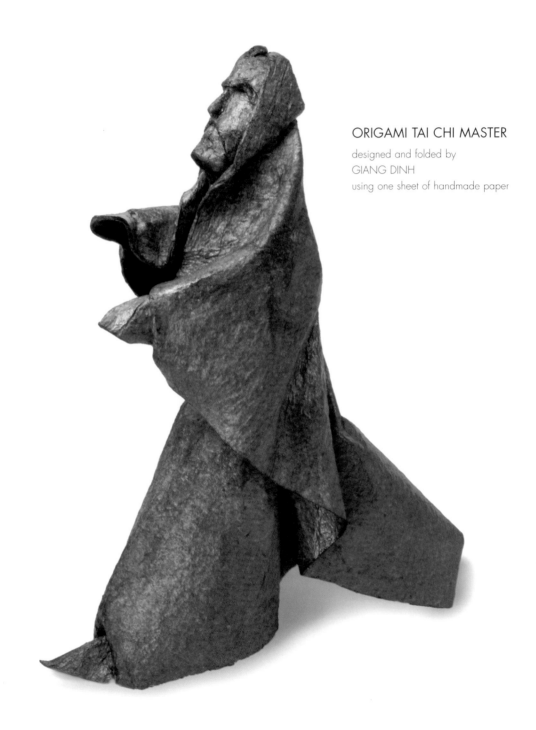

ORIGAMI TAI CHI MASTER
designed and folded by
GIANG DINH
using one sheet of handmade paper

MARCH 2004
S	M	T	W	T	F	S
	1	2	3	4	5	6
7	8	9	10	11	12	13
14	15	16	17	18	19	20
21	22	23	24	25	26	27
28	29	30	31			

MONDAY 8

International Women's Day
Labour Day (Australia—VIC)
Canberra Day (Australia—ACT)
Commonwealth Day (Australia, Canada, NZ, UK)

TUESDAY 9

WEDNESDAY 10

THURSDAY 11

FRIDAY 12

SATURDAY 13

SUNDAY 14

ORIGAMI ANCIENT WYRM

designed and folded by
JOSEPH WU
using two sheets of paper

MARCH 2004

S M T W T F S
       1 2 3 4 5 6
7 8 9 10 11 12 13
14 15 16 17 18 19 20
21 22 23 24 25 26 27
28 29 30 31

MARCH

MONDAY

15

TUESDAY

16

WEDNESDAY

17

St. Patrick's Day

THURSDAY

18

FRIDAY

19

SATURDAY

20

SUNDAY

21

Mothering Sunday (UK)

ORIGAMI UNICORN
designed and folded by
JOSEPH WU
using two sheets of paper

MARCH 2004

S	M	T	W	T	F	S
	1	2	3	4	5	6
7	8	9	10	11	12	13
14	15	16	17	18	19	20
21	22	23	24	25	26	27
28	29	30	31			

MONDAY 22

TUESDAY 23

WEDNESDAY 24

THURSDAY 25

FRIDAY 26

SATURDAY 27

SUNDAY 28

ORIGAMI COELOPHYSIS

designed and folded by
SATOSHI KAMIYA
using one sheet of handmade paper

MARCH 2004						
S	M	T	W	T	F	S
	1	2	3	4	5	6
7	8	9	10	11	12	13
14	15	16	17	18	19	20
21	22	23	24	25	26	27
28	29	30	31			

APRIL 2004						
S	M	T	W	T	F	S
				1	2	3
4	5	6	7	8	9	10
11	12	13	14	15	16	17
18	19	20	21	22	23	24
25	26	27	28	29	30	

MARCH/APRIL

MONDAY 29

TUESDAY 30

WEDNESDAY 31

THURSDAY 1

FRIDAY 2

SATURDAY 3

SUNDAY 4

Palm Sunday

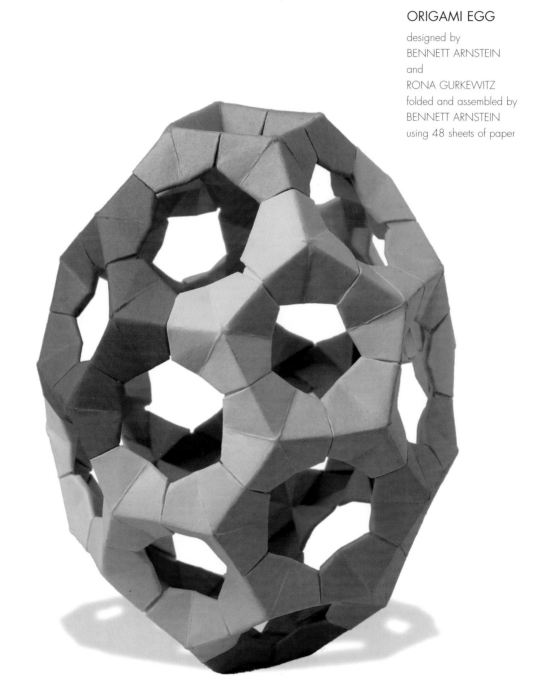

ORIGAMI EGG

designed by
BENNETT ARNSTEIN
and
RONA GURKEWITZ
folded and assembled by
BENNETT ARNSTEIN
using 48 sheets of paper

APRIL 2004

S	M	T	W	T	F	S
				1	2	3
4	5	6	7	8	9	10
11	12	13	14	15	16	17
18	19	20	21	22	23	24
25	26	27	28	29	30	

APRIL

MONDAY 5

TUESDAY 6

First Day of Passover

WEDNESDAY 7

THURSDAY 8

FRIDAY 9

Good Friday (Western, Orthodox)

SATURDAY 10

Easter Saturday (Australia—except VIC, WA)

SUNDAY 11

Easter (Western, Orthodox)

ORIGAMI FORTUNE TELLER

a traditional form folded by
V'ANN CORNELIUS
using one sheet of paper

APRIL 2004

S	M	T	W	T	F	S
				1	2	3
4	5	6	7	8	9	10
11	12	13	14	15	16	17
18	19	20	21	22	23	24
25	26	27	28	29	30	

APRIL

MONDAY   12

Easter Monday (Australia, Canada, NZ, UK—except Scotland)

TUESDAY   13

Last Day of Passover

WEDNESDAY   14

Bank Holiday (Australia—TAS)

THURSDAY   15

FRIDAY   16

SATURDAY   17

SUNDAY   18

ORIGAMI BAHAMUT
designed and folded by
SATOSHI KAMIYA
using one sheet of handmade paper

APRIL 2004

S	M	T	W	T	F	S
				1	2	3
4	5	6	7	8	9	10
11	12	13	14	15	16	17
18	19	20	21	22	23	24
25	26	27	28	29	30	

MONDAY   19

TUESDAY   20

WEDNESDAY   21

THURSDAY   22

Earth Day

FRIDAY   23

St. George's Day (UK)

SATURDAY   24   SUNDAY   25

APRIL 2004

S	M	T	W	T	F	S
				1	2	3
4	5	6	7	8	9	10
11	12	13	14	15	16	17
18	19	20	21	22	23	24
25	26	27	28	29	30	

MAY 2004

S	M	T	W	T	F	S
						1
2	3	4	5	6	7	8
9	10	11	12	13	14	15
16	17	18	19	20	21	22
23	24	25	26	27	28	29
30	31					

MONDAY — 26

Anzac Day (observed) (Australia, NZ)

TUESDAY — 27

WEDNESDAY — 28

THURSDAY — 29

FRIDAY — 30

SATURDAY — 1

SUNDAY — 2

ORIGAMI RABBIT

designed and folded by
JOSEPH WU
using two sheets of paper

MAY 2004

S	M	T	W	T	F	S
						1
2	3	4	5	6	7	8
9	10	11	12	13	14	15
16	17	18	19	20	21	22
23	24	25	26	27	28	29
30	31					

MAY

MONDAY   3

Labour Day (Australia—QLD)
Bank Holiday (Eire, UK)

TUESDAY   4

WEDNESDAY   5

THURSDAY   6

FRIDAY   7

SATURDAY   8

SUNDAY   9

Mother's Day (USA, Australia, Canada, NZ)

ORIGAMI SHELL
designed by
TOSHIKAZU KAWASAKI
folded by
PHILLIP YEE
using one piece of paper

MAY 2004

S	M	T	W	T	F	S
						1
2	3	4	5	6	7	8
9	10	11	12	13	14	15
16	17	18	19	20	21	22
23	24	25	26	27	28	29
30	31					

MONDAY 10

TUESDAY 11

WEDNESDAY 12

THURSDAY 13

FRIDAY 14

SATURDAY 15

SUNDAY 16

Armed Forces Day (USA)

ORIGAMI ANGEL

designed and folded by
JOSEPH WU

using three sheets of paper

MAY 2004

S	M	T	W	T	F	S
						1
2	3	4	5	6	7	8
9	10	11	12	13	14	15
16	17	18	19	20	21	22
23	24	25	26	27	28	29
30	31					

MONDAY 17

TUESDAY 18

WEDNESDAY 19

THURSDAY 20

Ascension

FRIDAY 21

SATURDAY 22

SUNDAY 23

ORIGAMI LILY

A traditional form folded by
V'ANN CORNELIUS
using one sheet of paper

MAY 2004

S	M	T	W	T	F	S
						1
2	3	4	5	6	7	8
9	10	11	12	13	14	15
16	17	18	19	20	21	22
23	24	25	26	27	28	29
30	31					

MONDAY 24

Victoria Day (Canada)

TUESDAY 25

WEDNESDAY 26

Shavuot begins

THURSDAY 27

Shavuot ends

FRIDAY 28

SATURDAY 29

SUNDAY 30

Whitsunday

ORIGAMI GYROSCOPED EGG

designed by
BENNETT ARNSTEIN
and
RONA GURKEWITZ
folded and assembled by
BENNETT ARNSTEIN
using 24 sheets of paper

MAY 2004

S	M	T	W	T	F	S
						1
2	3	4	5	6	7	8
9	10	11	12	13	14	15
16	17	18	19	20	21	22
23	24	25	26	27	28	29
30	31					

JUNE 2004

S	M	T	W	T	F	S
		1	2	3	4	5
6	7	8	9	10	11	12
13	14	15	16	17	18	19
20	21	22	23	24	25	26
27	28	29	30			

MONDAY — 31

Memorial Day (USA)
Bank Holiday (UK)

TUESDAY — 1

WEDNESDAY — 2

THURSDAY — 3

FRIDAY — 4

SATURDAY — 5

SUNDAY — 6

ORIGAMI SHARK

designed by
JOHN MONTROLL
folded by
PHILLIP YEE
using one sheet of paper

JUNE 2004

S	M	T	W	T	F	S
		1	2	3	4	5
6	7	8	9	10	11	12
13	14	15	16	17	18	19
20	21	22	23	24	25	26
27	28	29	30			

JUNE

MONDAY 7

Queen's Birthday (NZ)
Foundation Day (Australia—WA)
Bank Holiday (Eire)

TUESDAY 8

WEDNESDAY 9

THURSDAY 10

Corpus Christi

FRIDAY 11

SATURDAY 12

SUNDAY 13

ORIGAMI PEGASUS

designed and folded by
FUMIAKI KAWAHATA
using one sheet of paper

JUNE 2004

S	M	T	W	T	F	S
		1	2	3	4	5
6	7	8	9	10	11	12
13	14	15	16	17	18	19
20	21	22	23	24	25	26
27	28	29	30			

JUNE

MONDAY 14

Flag Day (USA)
Queen's Birthday (Australia—except WA)

TUESDAY 15

WEDNESDAY 16

THURSDAY 17

FRIDAY 18

SATURDAY 19

SUNDAY 20

Father's Day (USA, Canada, UK)

ORIGAMI KABUTO MUSHI

designed and folded by
ROBERT LANG
using one sheet of paper

JUNE 2004

S	M	T	W	T	F	S
		1	2	3	4	5
6	7	8	9	10	11	12
13	14	15	16	17	18	19
20	21	22	23	24	25	26
27	28	29	30			

JUNE

MONDAY   21

TUESDAY   22

WEDNESDAY   23

THURSDAY   24

FRIDAY   25

SATURDAY   26   SUNDAY   27

JUNE 2004

S	M	T	W	T	F	S
		1	2	3	4	5
6	7	8	9	10	11	12
13	14	15	16	17	18	19
20	21	22	23	24	25	26
27	28	29	30			

JULY 2004

S	M	T	W	T	F	S
				1	2	3
4	5	6	7	8	9	10
11	12	13	14	15	16	17
18	19	20	21	22	23	24
25	26	27	28	29	30	31

MONDAY   28

TUESDAY   29

WEDNESDAY   30

THURSDAY   1

Canada Day

FRIDAY   2

SATURDAY   3   SUNDAY   4

Independence Day (USA)

ORIGAMI HORSE

designed and folded by
ERIC JOISEL
using one sheet of foil-backed paper

JULY 2004

S	M	T	W	T	F	S
				1	2	3
4	5	6	7	8	9	10
11	12	13	14	15	16	17
18	19	20	21	22	23	24
25	26	27	28	29	30	31

JULY

MONDAY   5

TUESDAY   6

WEDNESDAY   7

THURSDAY   8

FRIDAY   9

SATURDAY   10   SUNDAY   11

ORIGAMI WESTERN POND TURTLE
designed and folded by
ROBERT LANG
using one sheet of paper

JULY 2004

S	M	T	W	T	F	S
				1	2	3
4	5	6	7	8	9	10
11	12	13	14	15	16	17
18	19	20	21	22	23	24
25	26	27	28	29	30	31

MONDAY 12

Battle of the Boyne Day (Northern Ireland)

TUESDAY 13

WEDNESDAY 14

THURSDAY 15

FRIDAY 16

SATURDAY 17

SUNDAY 18

ORIGAMI HIPPOCAMPUS
designed and folded by
JOSEPH WU
using three sheets of paper

JULY 2004

S	M	T	W	T	F	S
				1	2	3
4	5	6	7	8	9	10
11	12	13	14	15	16	17
18	19	20	21	22	23	24
25	26	27	28	29	30	31

JULY

MONDAY	19

TUESDAY	20

WEDNESDAY	21

THURSDAY	22

FRIDAY	23

SATURDAY	24	SUNDAY	25

ORIGAMI PTERANADON
designed and folded by
SATOSHI KAMIYA
using one sheet of handmade paper

JULY 2004

S	M	T	W	T	F	S
				1	2	3
4	5	6	7	8	9	10
11	12	13	14	15	16	17
18	19	20	21	22	23	24
25	26	27	28	29	30	31

AUGUST 2004

S	M	T	W	T	F	S
1	2	3	4	5	6	7
8	9	10	11	12	13	14
15	16	17	18	19	20	21
22	23	24	25	26	27	28
29	30	31				

JULY/AUGUST

MONDAY   26

TUESDAY   27

WEDNESDAY   28

THURSDAY   29

FRIDAY   30

SATURDAY   31   SUNDAY   1

ORIGAMI CRANE

designed and folded by
ERIC JOISEL
using one sheet of paper

AUGUST 2004

S	M	T	W	T	F	S
1	2	3	4	5	6	7
8	9	10	11	12	13	14
15	16	17	18	19	20	21
22	23	24	25	26	27	28
29	30	31				

AUGUST

MONDAY 2

Bank Holiday (Eire, Scotland, Australia—NSW, ACT)
Picnic Day (Australia—NT)

TUESDAY 3

WEDNESDAY 4

THURSDAY 5

FRIDAY 6

SATURDAY 7

SUNDAY 8

ORIGAMI SEREN'S HORSE

designed and folded by
JOSEPH WU
using two sheets of paper

AUGUST 2004

S	M	T	W	T	F	S
1	2	3	4	5	6	7
8	9	10	11	12	13	14
15	16	17	18	19	20	21
22	23	24	25	26	27	28
29	30	31				

AUGUST

MONDAY 9

TUESDAY 10

WEDNESDAY 11

THURSDAY 12

FRIDAY 13

SATURDAY 14

SUNDAY 15

Assumption

ORIGAMI FROG

A traditional form folded by
V'ANN CORNELIUS
using one sheet of paper

AUGUST 2004

S	M	T	W	T	F	S
1	2	3	4	5	6	7
8	9	10	11	12	13	14
15	16	17	18	19	20	21
22	23	24	25	26	27	28
29	30	31				

AUGUST

MONDAY 16

TUESDAY 17

WEDNESDAY 18

THURSDAY 19

FRIDAY 20

SATURDAY 21

SUNDAY 22

ORIGAMI KOI

designed and folded by
MICHAEL LA FOSSE
using one sheet of handmade paper

AUGUST 2004

S	M	T	W	T	F	S
1	2	3	4	5	6	7
8	9	10	11	12	13	14
15	16	17	18	19	20	21
22	23	24	25	26	27	28
29	30	31				

AUGUST

MONDAY 23

TUESDAY 24

WEDNESDAY 25

THURSDAY 26

FRIDAY 27

SATURDAY 28

SUNDAY 29

ORIGAMI UNICORN
designed and folded by
FUMIAKI KAWAHATA
using one sheet of paper

AUGUST 2004

S	M	T	W	T	F	S
1	2	3	4	5	6	7
8	9	10	11	12	13	14
15	16	17	18	19	20	21
22	23	24	25	26	27	28
29	30	31				

SEPTEMBER 2004

S	M	T	W	T	F	S
			1	2	3	4
5	6	7	8	9	10	11
12	13	14	15	16	17	18
19	20	21	22	23	24	25
26	27	28	29	30		

MONDAY 30

Bank Holiday (UK—except Scotland)

TUESDAY 31

WEDNESDAY 1

THURSDAY 2

FRIDAY 3

SATURDAY 4

SUNDAY 5

Father's Day (Australia, NZ)

ORIGAMI STAR

designed by
NINA OSTRUN
folded and assembled by
V'ANN CORNELIUS
using eight sheets of paper

SEPTEMBER 2004

S	M	T	W	T	F	S
			1	2	3	4
5	6	7	8	9	10	11
12	13	14	15	16	17	18
19	20	21	22	23	24	25
26	27	28	29	30		

SEPTEMBER

MONDAY   6

Labor Day (USA, Canada)

TUESDAY   7

WEDNESDAY   8

THURSDAY   9

FRIDAY   10

SATURDAY   11   SUNDAY   12

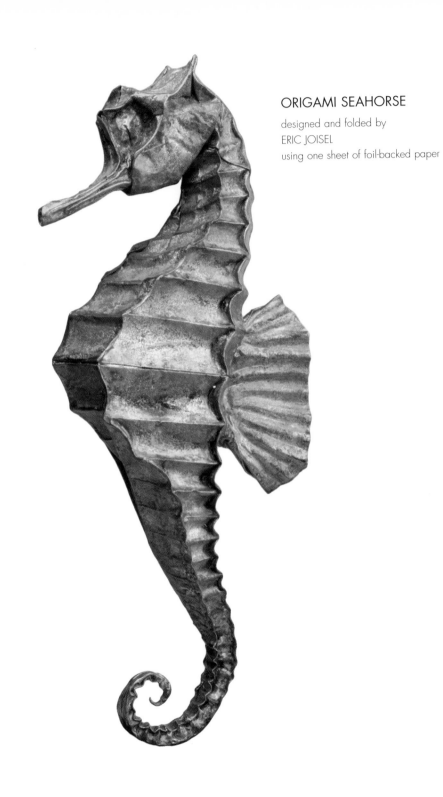

ORIGAMI SEAHORSE
designed and folded by
ERIC JOISEL
using one sheet of foil-backed paper

SEPTEMBER 2004

S	M	T	W	T	F	S
			1	2	3	4
5	6	7	8	9	10	11
12	13	14	15	16	17	18
19	20	21	22	23	24	25
26	27	28	29	30		

MONDAY 13

TUESDAY 14

WEDNESDAY 15

THURSDAY 16

Rosh Hashanah begins

FRIDAY 17

Rosh Hashanah ends

SATURDAY 18

SUNDAY 19

ORIGAMI TREE

designed and folded by
VINCENT FLODERER

using one sheet of French wrapping paper

SEPTEMBER 2004

S	M	T	W	T	F	S
			1	2	3	4
5	6	7	8	9	10	11
12	13	14	15	16	17	18
19	20	21	22	23	24	25
26	27	28	29	30		

SEPTEMBER

MONDAY 20

TUESDAY 21

WEDNESDAY 22

THURSDAY 23

FRIDAY 24

SATURDAY 25

SUNDAY 26

Yom Kippur

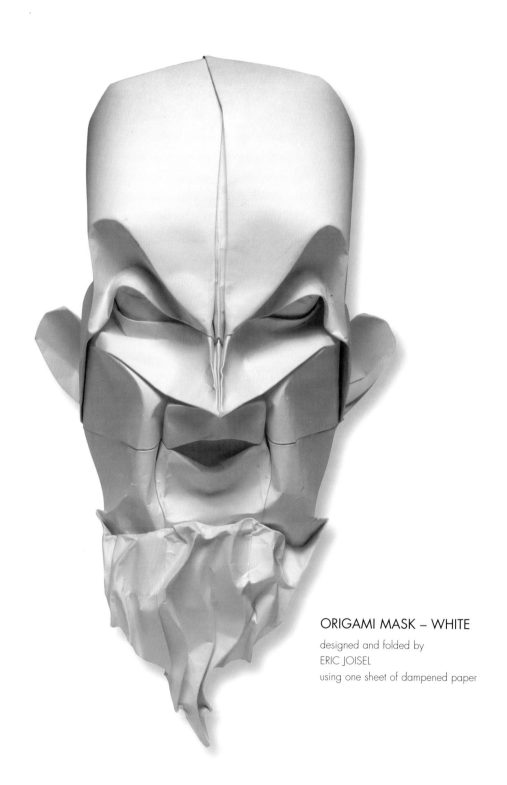

ORIGAMI MASK – WHITE

designed and folded by
ERIC JOISEL
using one sheet of dampened paper

SEPTEMBER 2004

S	M	T	W	T	F	S
			1	2	3	4
5	6	7	8	9	10	11
12	13	14	15	16	17	18
19	20	21	22	23	24	25
26	27	28	29	30		

OCTOBER 2004

S	M	T	W	T	F	S
					1	2
3	4	5	6	7	8	9
10	11	12	13	14	15	16
17	18	19	20	21	22	23
24	25	26	27	28	29	30
31						

MONDAY 27

Queen's Birthday (Australia — WA)

TUESDAY 28

WEDNESDAY 29

THURSDAY 30

First Day of Tabernacles

FRIDAY 1

Second Day of Tabernacles

SATURDAY 2

SUNDAY 3

ORIGAMI DIMETRADON
designed and folded by
FUMIAKI KAWAHATA
using one sheet of paper

OCTOBER 2004

S	M	T	W	T	F	S
					1	2
3	4	5	6	7	8	9
10	11	12	13	14	15	16
17	18	19	20	21	22	23
24	25	26	27	28	29	30
31						

OCTOBER

MONDAY 4

Labour Day (Australia—ACT, NSW, SA)

TUESDAY 5

WEDNESDAY 6

THURSDAY 7

FRIDAY 8

SATURDAY 9

SUNDAY 10

ORIGAMI BLACK BEAR

designed and folded by
JOSEPH WU
using one sheet of paper

OCTOBER 2004

S	M	T	W	T	F	S
					1	2
3	4	5	6	7	8	9
10	11	12	13	14	15	16
17	18	19	20	21	22	23
24	25	26	27	28	29	30
31						

MONDAY 11

Columbus Day (USA)
Thanksgiving (Canada)

TUESDAY 12

WEDNESDAY 13

THURSDAY 14

FRIDAY 15

SATURDAY 16

SUNDAY 17

ORIGAMI BULL MOOSE

designed and folded by
ROBERT LANG
using one sheet of paper with a separate base

OCTOBER 2004

S	M	T	W	T	F	S
					1	2
3	4	5	6	7	8	9
10	11	12	13	14	15	16
17	18	19	20	21	22	23
24	25	26	27	28	29	30
31						

OCTOBER

MONDAY 18

TUESDAY 19

WEDNESDAY 20

THURSDAY 21

FRIDAY 22

SATURDAY 23

SUNDAY 24

United Nations Day

ORIGAMI GOBLIN

designed and folded by
JOSEPH WU
using two sheets of paper

OCTOBER 2004

S	M	T	W	T	F	S
					1	2
3	4	5	6	7	8	9
10	11	12	13	14	15	16
17	18	19	20	21	22	23
24	25	26	27	28	29	30
31						

MONDAY 25

Labour Day (NZ)
Bank Holiday (Eire)

TUESDAY 26

WEDNESDAY 27

THURSDAY 28

FRIDAY 29

SATURDAY 30

SUNDAY 31

Halloween

ORIGAMI PLEAT FORM 1
designed and folded by
FLORENCE TEMKO
using one sheet of paper

NOVEMBER 2004

S	M	T	W	T	F	S
	1	2	3	4	5	6
7	8	9	10	11	12	13
14	15	16	17	18	19	20
21	22	23	24	25	26	27
28	29	30				

NOVEMBER

MONDAY 1

All Saints' Day

TUESDAY 2

Election Day (USA)
All Souls' Day

WEDNESDAY 3

THURSDAY 4

FRIDAY 5

SATURDAY 6

SUNDAY 7

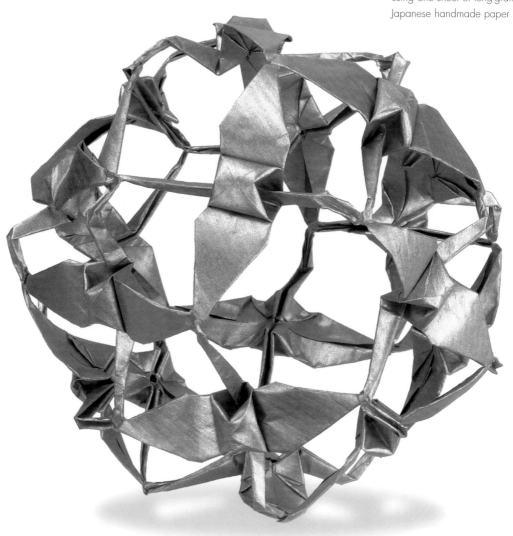

ORIGAMI CRANE ORB

designed and folded by
LINDA MIHARA
using one sheet of long-grain
Japanese handmade paper

NOVEMBER 2004

S	M	T	W	T	F	S
	1	2	3	4	5	6
7	8	9	10	11	12	13
14	15	16	17	18	19	20
21	22	23	24	25	26	27
28	29	30				

NOVEMBER

MONDAY 8

TUESDAY 9

WEDNESDAY 10

THURSDAY 11

Veterans' Day (USA)
Remembrance Day (Canada, UK)

FRIDAY 12

SATURDAY 13

SUNDAY 14

ORIGAMI CHINESE VASE

a traditional form folded by
V'ANN CORNELIUS
using one sheet of paper

NOVEMBER 2004

S	M	T	W	T	F	S
	1	2	3	4	5	6
7	8	9	10	11	12	13
14	15	16	17	18	19	20
21	22	23	24	25	26	27
28	29	30				

NOVEMBER

MONDAY   15

TUESDAY   16

WEDNESDAY   17

THURSDAY   18

FRIDAY   19

SATURDAY   20   SUNDAY   21

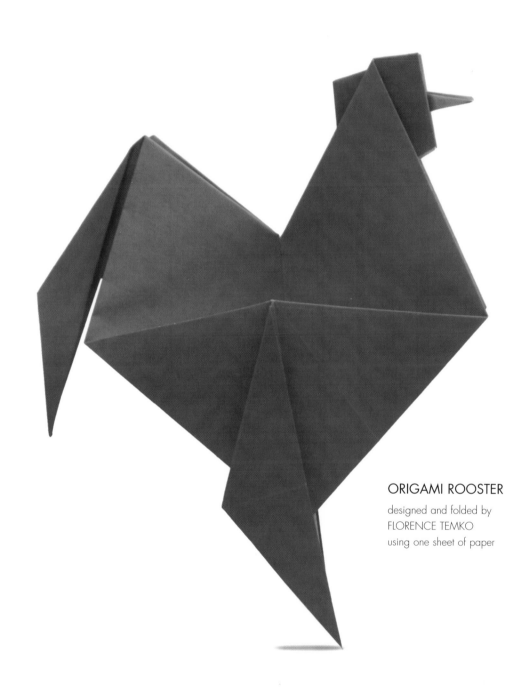

ORIGAMI ROOSTER

designed and folded by
FLORENCE TEMKO
using one sheet of paper

NOVEMBER 2004

S	M	T	W	T	F	S
	1	2	3	4	5	6
7	8	9	10	11	12	13
14	15	16	17	18	19	20
21	22	23	24	25	26	27
28	29	30				

NOVEMBER

MONDAY   22

TUESDAY   23

WEDNESDAY   24

THURSDAY   25

Thanksgiving (USA)

FRIDAY   26

SATURDAY   27   SUNDAY   28

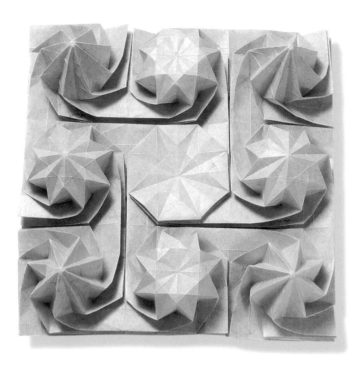

ORIGAMI TESSELATION 2A

designed and folded by
CHRIS PALMER
using one sheet of paper

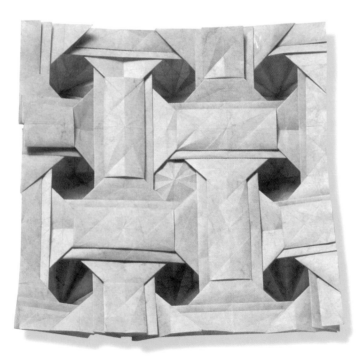

ORIGAMI TESSELATION 2B

designed and folded by
CHRIS PALMER
using one sheet of paper

NOVEMBER 2004

S	M	T	W	T	F	S
	1	2	3	4	5	6
7	8	9	10	11	12	13
14	15	16	17	18	19	20
21	22	23	24	25	26	27
28	29	30				

DECEMBER 2004

S	M	T	W	T	F	S
			1	2	3	4
5	6	7	8	9	10	11
12	13	14	15	16	17	18
19	20	21	22	23	24	25
26	27	28	29	30	31	

MONDAY   29

TUESDAY   30

St. Andrew's Day (UK)

WEDNESDAY   1

THURSDAY   2

FRIDAY   3

SATURDAY   4   SUNDAY   5

DECEMBER 2004

S	M	T	W	T	F	S
			1	2	3	4
5	6	7	8	9	10	11
12	13	14	15	16	17	18
19	20	21	22	23	24	25
26	27	28	29	30	31	

DECEMBER

MONDAY 6

TUESDAY 7

WEDNESDAY 8

First Day of Hanukkah

THURSDAY 9

FRIDAY 10

Human Rights Day

SATURDAY 11

SUNDAY 12

ORIGAMI ANGEL WITH A LUTE

designed and folded by
FUMIAKI KAWAHATA

using one sheet of paper

DECEMBER 2004

S	M	T	W	T	F	S
			1	2	3	4
5	6	7	8	9	10	11
12	13	14	15	16	17	18
19	20	21	22	23	24	25
26	27	28	29	30	31	

MONDAY   13

TUESDAY   14

WEDNESDAY   15

Last Day of Hanukkah

THURSDAY   16

FRIDAY   17

SATURDAY   18   SUNDAY   19

ORIGAMI RINGS

designed, folded, and assembled by
BENNETT ARNSTEIN
using 240 sheets of paper

DECEMBER 2004

S	M	T	W	T	F	S
			1	2	3	4
5	6	7	8	9	10	11
12	13	14	15	16	17	18
19	20	21	22	23	24	25
26	27	28	29	30	31	

DECEMBER

MONDAY 20

TUESDAY 21

WEDNESDAY 22

THURSDAY 23

FRIDAY 24

Christmas Eve

SATURDAY 25

Christmas Day

SUNDAY 26

Kwanzaa begins (USA)
Boxing Day (Canada, NZ, UK, Australia—except SA)
Proclamation Day (Australia—SA)

ORIGAMI STAR-BLINTZ

A traditional form folded by
V'ANN CORNELIUS
using one sheet of paper

DECEMBER 2004

S	M	T	W	T	F	S
			1	2	3	4
5	6	7	8	9	10	11
12	13	14	15	16	17	18
19	20	21	22	23	24	25
26	27	28	29	30	31	

JANUARY 2005

S	M	T	W	T	F	S
						1
2	3	4	5	6	7	8
9	10	11	12	13	14	15
16	17	18	19	20	21	22
23	24	25	26	27	28	29
30	31					

MONDAY 27

TUESDAY 28

WEDNESDAY 29

THURSDAY 30

FRIDAY 31

SATURDAY 1

New Year's Day
Kwanzaa ends (USA)

SUNDAY 2

2005

JANUARY

FEBRUARY

MARCH

APRIL

MAY

JUNE

2005

JULY

AUGUST

SEPTEMBER

OCTOBER

NOVEMBER

DECEMBER

2003

JANUARY
S	M	T	W	T	F	S
			1	2	3	4
5	6	7	8	9	10	11
12	13	14	15	16	17	18
19	20	21	22	23	24	25
26	27	28	29	30	31	

FEBRUARY
S	M	T	W	T	F	S
						1
2	3	4	5	6	7	8
9	10	11	12	13	14	15
16	17	18	19	20	21	22
23	24	25	26	27	28	

MARCH
S	M	T	W	T	F	S
						1
2	3	4	5	6	7	8
9	10	11	12	13	14	15
16	17	18	19	20	21	22
23	24	25	26	27	28	29
30	31					

APRIL
S	M	T	W	T	F	S
		1	2	3	4	5
6	7	8	9	10	11	12
13	14	15	16	17	18	19
20	21	22	23	24	25	26
27	28	29	30			

MAY
S	M	T	W	T	F	S
				1	2	3
4	5	6	7	8	9	10
11	12	13	14	15	16	17
18	19	20	21	22	23	24
25	26	27	28	29	30	31

JUNE
S	M	T	W	T	F	S
1	2	3	4	5	6	7
8	9	10	11	12	13	14
15	16	17	18	19	20	21
22	23	24	25	26	27	28
29	30					

JULY
S	M	T	W	T	F	S
		1	2	3	4	5
6	7	8	9	10	11	12
13	14	15	16	17	18	19
20	21	22	23	24	25	26
27	28	29	30	31		

AUGUST
S	M	T	W	T	F	S
					1	2
3	4	5	6	7	8	9
10	11	12	13	14	15	16
17	18	19	20	21	22	23
24	25	26	27	28	29	30
31						

SEPTEMBER
S	M	T	W	T	F	S
	1	2	3	4	5	6
7	8	9	10	11	12	13
14	15	16	17	18	19	20
21	22	23	24	25	26	27
28	29	30				

OCTOBER
S	M	T	W	T	F	S
			1	2	3	4
5	6	7	8	9	10	11
12	13	14	15	16	17	18
19	20	21	22	23	24	25
26	27	28	29	30	31	

NOVEMBER
S	M	T	W	T	F	S
						1
2	3	4	5	6	7	8
9	10	11	12	13	14	15
16	17	18	19	20	21	22
23	24	25	26	27	28	29
30						

DECEMBER
S	M	T	W	T	F	S
	1	2	3	4	5	6
7	8	9	10	11	12	13
14	15	16	17	18	19	20
21	22	23	24	25	26	27
28	29	30	31			

2005

JANUARY
S	M	T	W	T	F	S
						1
2	3	4	5	6	7	8
9	10	11	12	13	14	15
16	17	18	19	20	21	22
23	24	25	26	27	28	29
30	31					

FEBRUARY
S	M	T	W	T	F	S
		1	2	3	4	5
6	7	8	9	10	11	12
13	14	15	16	17	18	19
20	21	22	23	24	25	26
27	28					

MARCH
S	M	T	W	T	F	S
		1	2	3	4	5
6	7	8	9	10	11	12
13	14	15	16	17	18	19
20	21	22	23	24	25	26
27	28	29	30	31		

APRIL
S	M	T	W	T	F	S
					1	2
3	4	5	6	7	8	9
10	11	12	13	14	15	16
17	18	19	20	21	22	23
24	25	26	27	28	29	30

MAY
S	M	T	W	T	F	S
1	2	3	4	5	6	7
8	9	10	11	12	13	14
15	16	17	18	19	20	21
22	23	24	25	26	27	28
29	30	31				

JUNE
S	M	T	W	T	F	S
			1	2	3	4
5	6	7	8	9	10	11
12	13	14	15	16	17	18
19	20	21	22	23	24	25
26	27	28	29	30		

JULY
S	M	T	W	T	F	S
					1	2
3	4	5	6	7	8	9
10	11	12	13	14	15	16
17	18	19	20	21	22	23
24	25	26	27	28	29	30
31						

AUGUST
S	M	T	W	T	F	S
	1	2	3	4	5	6
7	8	9	10	11	12	13
14	15	16	17	18	19	20
21	22	23	24	25	26	27
28	29	30	31			

SEPTEMBER
S	M	T	W	T	F	S
				1	2	3
4	5	6	7	8	9	10
11	12	13	14	15	16	17
18	19	20	21	22	23	24
25	26	27	28	29	30	

OCTOBER
S	M	T	W	T	F	S
						1
2	3	4	5	6	7	8
9	10	11	12	13	14	15
16	17	18	19	20	21	22
23	24	25	26	27	28	29
30	31					

NOVEMBER
S	M	T	W	T	F	S
		1	2	3	4	5
6	7	8	9	10	11	12
13	14	15	16	17	18	19
20	21	22	23	24	25	26
27	28	29	30			

DECEMBER
S	M	T	W	T	F	S
				1	2	3
4	5	6	7	8	9	10
11	12	13	14	15	16	17
18	19	20	21	22	23	24
25	26	27	28	29	30	31